# STC Guard Card Training®

**Guard Card TRAINING**

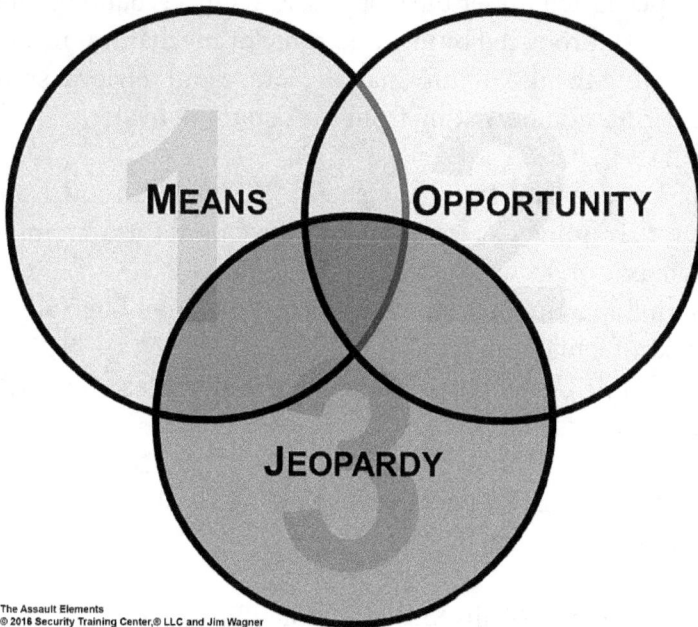

- MEANS
- OPPORTUNITY
- JEOPARDY

The Assault Elements
© 2016 Security Training Center,® LLC and Jim Wagner

# Use of Force

**Security TRAINING CENTER, LLC.**

Published by

**Security Training Center,® LLC.**
6520 PLATT AVE #174
WEST HILLS, CA 91307-3218
Security-Training-Center.com
(855) 500-3633

Trademarks: "Security Training Center", "STC Guard Card Training", the Security Training Center Logo, and the Guard Card Training logo are trademarks of Security Training Center,® LLC.
"Palladium Education" and the Palladium Education Logo are trademarks of Palladium Education,® Inc.
"War Arts" and "Use of Force Ladder" are trademarks of Jim Wagner Reality-Based Personal Protection.

Special thanks to Jim Wagner for permission to use his material in this coursework.

Jim Wagner Reality-Based Personal Protection
www.JimWagnerRealityBased.com


ISBN-13:     978-1-939408-46-4
ISBN-10:     1-939408-46-6

10 9 8 7 6 5 4 3 2

# Use of Force

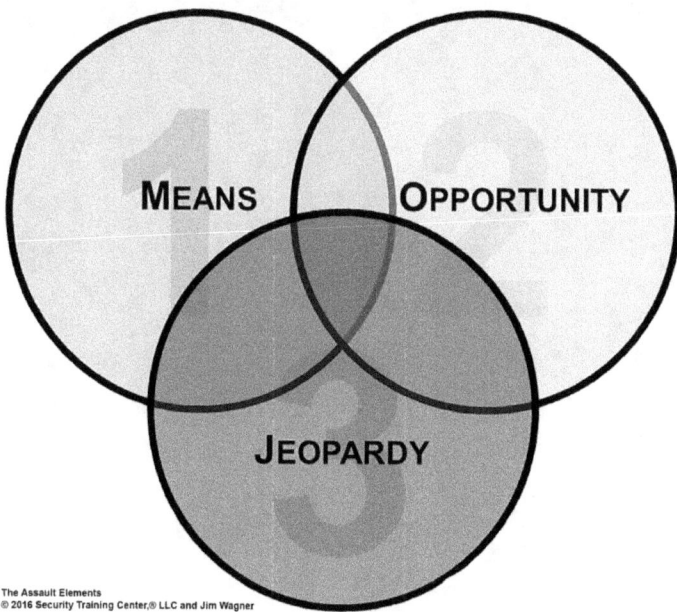

MEANS

OPPORTUNITY

JEOPARDY

The Assault Elements
© 2016 Security Training Center,® LLC and Jim Wagner

Jim Wagner
Author

Alex Haddox, M.Ed.
Author

William Green, M.Ed.
Editor in Chief

# Disclaimer

Security Training Center,* LLC. offers course material for training and certification. It is up to the student to complete the training within the mandatory timeframe as required by the state licensing agency. Security Training Center,* LLC. and its parent companies accept no responsibility for loss of licensure, registration, employment or fines resulting from failure of the student to complete the training within the timeframes specified by the state licensing agency.

Security Training Center,* LLC. and its parent companies **will not** notify or remind students of training deadlines. It is up to the individual to maintain personal professional training records, credentials and schedule of courses.

The material contained within this manual is the sole creation of Security Training Center,* LLC. which holds the copyright hereto. It is not official State-created training material.

Security Training Center,® LLC.

# Notice of Liability

The information in these programs is distributed without warranty. While every precaution has been taken in the preparation of this program, neither the author, Security Training Center,® LLC. nor its parent companies shall have any liability to any person or entity with respect to any injury, loss, or damage caused or alleged to be caused directly or indirectly by the instructions contained in any program or by instruction provided by Security Training Center,® LLC.

# About Security Training Center, LLC.

Security Training Center, LLC. is a professional security guard training company. The mission of Security Training Center, LLC is to educate security personnel and organizations in the latest protocols and techniques to keep staff, property, and other valuables safe. A proactive approach to security awareness prevents many problems from occurring thereby reducing risk to staff and potential liability actions. The approach is to teach early identification of potential problems and how to defuse conflicts before reaching crisis. Security Training Center, LLC's staff and advisory board have decades of experience in military, law enforcement, executive protection, private security, defensive weapons and martial arts.

Not only does Security Training Center, LLC offer direct training, but also provides guard card training materials for use by other organizations. Many companies have highly trained and experienced individuals. Unfortunately these companies may lack the teaching experience or materials to be able to impart the knowledge. For situations like these, Security Training Center, LLC. offers pre-packaged STC Guard Card Training® materials. Security Training Center, LLC's team is comprised exclusively of education and security professionals, many of whom hold advanced degrees in Adult Education and Training.

STC Guard Card Training® materials are available in multiple formats to meet most any need:

- Instructor-led, classroom training
  Printed STC Guard Card Training® manuals, lecture notes, handouts and presentations
- Online, self-paced training
  Interactive guard card eLearning with audio, video and animations
- Podcasts
  Downloadable or streamable audio lectures, case studies and interviews
- Books
- YouTube videos
- DVDs

# Security Training Center,® LLC.
## 6520 PLATT AVE, #174
## WEST HILLS, CA 91307-3218
## Security-Training-Center.com
## (855) 500-3633

# Contents

# Objectives

By the end of this lesson, the student will be able to:

- Know the responsibilities of a private security guard
- Understand the appropriate use of reasonable force.
- Understand the Use of Force Continuum/Ladder.
- Understand the use of restraint techniques and their implications.
- Understand the use of deadly force.
- Understand the use of force in property defense.
- Understand escalation and de-escalation techniques in the use of force.

Security Training Center, LLC.

# Overview

Company-provided use of force policies supersedes all recommendations included in this training.

Laws, Penal Codes, Statutes and Jury Instructions from various states are quoted throughout this chapter as examples and general guidance. Every states has a specific set of rules, regulations and laws. The guard must always work within the local state laws, regulations and company policy.

Verbal deflection and de-escalation techniques are always the first line of defense and the use of physical force is a measure of last resort. A force-on-force encounter does not end when the act of violence ceases. The psychological impact of a physical attack can last a lifetime. Legal troubles, both civil and criminal, can linger for years or even decades. What follows is a brief explanation of generally accepted use of force legal standards.

There are specific rules on the appropriate use of force in making an arrest, personal protection, defense of another, defense of property, and other situations. Security guards are held to the civilian standard which differs from law enforcement or military. The guiding principle for use

Use of Force                                                                                       1 of force is a "reasonable amount of force." For comparison, sworn peace officers are allowed to use a "necessary amount of force" to execute their duty. Security guards are not peace officers and held to a more restrictive standard.

After a force-on-force encounter the security guard will be required to justify the use of force. Justification always falls under the "Reasonable Man Doctrine." The "Reasonable Man" is a hypothetical person representing what an "everyman" of average intelligence would believe to be true or how one would act at that exact moment with the information available at that moment. For example, how would a normal, average, "reasonable" person act in the same instance? The utmost discretion and caution must be employed when capturing, containing, or restraining a suspect.

---

The security guard is held to the private citizen standard. Rules and justifications that apply to sworn law enforcement **DO NOT** apply to private security guards.

---

# Definitions

| | |
|---|---|
| **Assault:** | An assault is an unlawful attempt, coupled with a present ability, to commit a violent injury on the person of another.[1] |
| **Battery:** | A battery is any willful and unlawful use of force or violence upon the person of another.[2] |
| **Great bodily injury:** | Significant or substantial physical injury. It is an injury that is greater than minor or moderate harm.[3] |
| **Homicide:** | The act of committing murder. |
| **Imminent peril:** | The peril must have existed or appeared to the defendant to have existed at the very time the fatal shot was fired. In other words, the peril must appear to the defendant as immediate and present and not prospective or even in |

---

1 California Penal Code 240
2 California Penal Code 242
3 CALCRIM No. 508

the near future. An imminent peril is one that, from appearances, must be instantly dealt with.[4]

**Murder:**   The unlawful killing of a human being, or a fetus, with malice aforethought.[5]

**Reasonable force:**   The amount of force that a reasonable person in the same situation would believe is necessary to protect the property from imminent harm.[6]

---

4   CALCRIM No. 505
5   California Penal Code, §187(a)
6   CALCRIM No. 3476

# Deprivation of Rights Under Color of Law

## Summary

Section 242 of Title 18 makes it a crime for a person acting under color of any law to willfully deprive a person of a right or privilege protected by the Constitution or laws of the United States.

For the purpose of Section 242, acts under "color of law" include acts not only done by federal, state, or local officials within the their lawful authority, but also acts done beyond the bounds of that official's lawful authority, if the acts are done while the official is purporting to or pretending to act in the performance of his/her official duties. Persons acting under color of law within the meaning of this statute include police officers, prisons guards and other law enforcement officials, as well as judges, care providers in public health facilities, and others who are acting as public officials. It is not necessary that the crime be motivated by animus toward the race, color, religion, sex, handicap, familial status or national origin of the victim.

The offense is punishable by a range of imprisonment up to a life term, or the death penalty, depending upon the circumstances of the crime, and the resulting injury, if any.

# Title 18, U.S.C., Section 242

Whoever, under color of any law, statute, ordinance, regulation, or custom, willfully subjects any person in any State, Territory, Commonwealth, Possession, or District to the deprivation of any rights, privileges, or immunities secured or protected by the Constitution or laws of the United States, ... shall be fined under this title or imprisoned not more than one year, or both; and if bodily injury results from the acts committed in violation of this section or if such acts include the use, attempted use, or threatened use of a dangerous weapon, explosives, or fire, shall be fined under this title or imprisoned not more than ten years, or both; and if death results from the acts committed in violation of this section or if such acts include kidnaping or an attempt to kidnap, aggravated sexual abuse, or an attempt to commit aggravated sexual abuse, or an attempt to kill, shall be fined under this title, or imprisoned for any term of years or for life, or both, or may be sentenced to death.[1]

---

1    The United States Department of Justice.
     http://www.justice.gov/crt/about/crm/242fin.php

# Fight versus Self-Defense

The claim of self-defense is reserved for those who are truly innocent. In self-defense, aggression is one-sided. In the two sides of a self-defense event there is an attacker and the other is an unwilling participant seeking to defend and escape. Defending oneself against an unprovoked attack is a fundamental human right.

In contrast, a fight is a cooperative force-on-force event. Most state laws refer to fighting as "mutual combat." The ancient adage "it takes two to fight" still holds true today. In a fight, neither side can claim self-defense as both entered into the physical altercation willingly. Unlicensed fighting is a crime and both parties may face criminal prosecution and civil lawsuits. Justifications for using physical force such as "because he was being a jerk" or "he deserved it" will most likely eliminate any claim to self-defense.

# Hawaii Revised Statutes Division 5. Crimes and Criminal Proceedings, §707-712, Assault in the third degree.

1. A person commits the offense of assault in the third degree if the person:
   a) Intentionally, knowingly, or recklessly causes bodily injury to another person; or
   b) Negligently causes bodily injury to another person with a dangerous instrument.
2. Assault in the third degree is a misdemeanor unless committed in a fight or scuffle entered into by mutual consent, in which case it is a petty misdemeanor.

Some schoolyard hypothetical examples to differentiate a fight versus self-defense follow.

**Example 1:**
If student 1, a bully, attacks student 2 to take his lunch money, student 2 would have the right to defend himself and his property with a claim to self-defense. Student 2 did not want his lunch money taken, nor did he seek out the bully to entice him to take his money. The event was one-sided, student 1 attacking student 2, thus a claim to self-defense is legitimate.

**Example 2:**
Student 1 and student 2 have a verbal altercation on the schoolyard. Student 1 tells student 2, "Meet me behind the gym, after school, at 3:15 and we'll settle this." If student 2 shows up at the time to "settle" the dispute with student 1, neither can claim self-defense. It was a predetermined meeting with an obvious agenda: a fight. A reasonable person not wanting to get into a physical conflict would not have showed up. Only a person who wanted to enter into the physical conflict would appear at the predetermined time and location. Thus, the desire to enter into a force-on-force encounter was mutual and neither side can claim self-defense.

Leaving the schoolyard behind, the following is a hypothetical road-rage example.

**Road Incident Example:**
Two men are driving along the freeway. Man 1 cuts off man 2. The two men exchange words, gestures, horn blowing and reckless, threatening driving. Both men exit the freeway, pull over to the side of the road, exit their vehicles and exchange more words. Things quickly escalate and the men exchange blows. A bystander witnesses the altercation and calls the police. When the police arrive, man 2 claims self-defense as man 1 initially cut him off on the freeway. Both men are arrested.

Both men were arrested as they both willingly entered into the physical altercation. Man 1 may have accidentally cutoff man 2, however, the reaction on both sides was excessive for the trigger event of a rude, perhaps even accidental, driving maneuver. Furthermore, it was obvious that both men wanted to fight, otherwise neither would have pulled over at the same time and place and exited their vehicles. A reasonable person wishing to avoid a physical altercation would have stayed on the road and notified law enforcement of a reckless driver making threatening motions on the freeway. A reasonable person would not have pulled off the road to directly confront the obviously angry and aggressive person. A reasonable person would have sought to avoid and escape the unstable individual. Therefore the result was a fight, not self-defense, and illegal. Thus, both men were arrested.

# Provoking an Attack

In many legal jurisdictions provoking an attack is cause to lose the claim to self-defense. This also negates the "…but he threw the first punch" self-defense claim.

Hawaii Revised Statutes Division 5. Crimes and Criminal Proceedings, §711-1106, Harassment.

1. A person commits the offense of harassment if, with intent to harass, annoy, or alarm any other person, that person:
   a) Strikes, shoves, kicks, or otherwise touches another person in an offensive manner or subjects the other person to offensive physical contact;
   b) Insults, taunts, or challenges another person in a manner likely to provoke an immediate violent response or that would cause the other person to reasonably believe that the actor intends to cause bodily injury to the recipient or another or damage to the property of the recipient or another;
   c) Repeatedly makes telephone calls, facsimile transmissions, or any form of electronic communication as defined in section 711-1111(2), including electronic mail transmissions, without purpose of legitimate communication;

d) Repeatedly makes a communication anonymously or at an extremely inconvenient hour;
e) Repeatedly makes communications, after being advised by the person to whom the communication is directed that further communication is unwelcome; or
f) Makes a communication using offensively coarse language that would cause the recipient to reasonably believe that the actor intends to cause bodily injury to the recipient or another or damage to the property of the recipient or another.

2. Harassment is a petty misdemeanor.

California Penal Code, Part 1. Of Crimes and Punishments, Title 11, of Crimes Against the Public Peace. §415.
Any of the following persons shall be punished by imprisonment in the county jail for a period of not more than 90 days, a fine of not more than four hundred dollars ($400), or both such imprisonment and fine:
1. Any person who unlawfully fights in a public place or challenges another person in a public place to fight.
2. Any person who maliciously and willfully disturbs another person by loud and unreasonable noise.
3. Any person who uses offensive words in a public place which are inherently likely to provoke an immediate violent reaction.

The following is a hypothetical example of provoking an attack.

> Man 1 is sitting on a stool at a bar. Man 2 approaches Man 1 and in a menacing tone says, "Hey, Jerkwad, You're sitting in my chair."
>
> Man 1 responds with, "I was here first. Piss off."
>
> Man 2 strikes Man 1 and a physical encounter ensues.

It can be argued that Man 1 provoked the attack. A reasonable person looking to avoid a physical confrontation would have found an alternative means to resolve the conflict including giving up the seat. Man 2 was being a bully. Man 1 was not legally required to give up his seat. However, Man 1's response was aggressive and provocative. Therefore, Man 1 might lose his right to claim self-defense if prosecuted.

Man 1 could have selected a different response and still retained his right to self-defense if attacked. For example, Man 1 could have said, "I'm sorry, Friend, but I've been here for a while now. Tell you what, let me buy you a drink to make up for it." In this example, Man 1 did not give up his seat, but did so in a non-inflammatory manner. In addition, he offered recompense for the alleged slight. In this case, if Man 2 still attacked Man 1, Man 1 would have a fair claim to self-defense.

In another example, an irate customer verbally assaults a sales associate and security guard.

> A sales associate calls for security when a customer becomes verbally abusive. The security guard walks up to the irate customer and asks, "What is going on here?"

> The customer responds with, "What does it look like? You guys are trying to rip me off. This clerk won't refund my money for this crap product I bought here."

> The sales associate sheepishly states, "He doesn't have his receipt. I can't process the return without a receipt."

> The security guard says, "Sir, there is nothing we can do without a receipt. It's against policy. You need to calm down or leave now."

> The customer, getting angrier still, turns to guard and says, "Screw policy. You give me my money back right now or I'll take it out of your hide."

> Staring the man down, the security guard growls, "Bring it."

In this example, the security guard missed several opportunities to diffuse a volatile situation. Subtle changes to wording, for instance changing a "no" response into solution could have served the escalating conflict more effectively. Most importantly, the moment the guard uttered, "Bring it," he lost all defensive credibility and invited an attack. That statement made it clear that all conversation was over and only a physical confrontation would proceed. After such a statement, the security guard could not claim self-defense or protection of others in a physical conflict. He was clearly welcoming a fight.

The following is an alternative means of handling the same customer while deescalating the conflict.

> A sales associate calls for security when a customer becomes verbally abusive. The security guard walks up to the sales associate and states, "Good morning, Beth. How can I help?"
>
> The customer interjects with, "Help? You guys are trying to rip me off. This clerk won't refund my money for this crap product I bought here."
>
> The sales associate sheepishly states, "He doesn't have his receipt. I can't process the return without a receipt."
>
> The security guard says, "Sir, we can absolutely process your return. All we need is the receipt. Do you have that with you?"
>
> The customer yells, "No, you idiot! Didn't you hear her? I don't have my receipt."
>
> Ignoring the insult, the security guard continues in a friendly tone. "I'm sorry. What was your name again? Bob? Bob, my name is Jack and I need your help. Can you help me out here?"
>
> The customer asks, "My help? What do you need my help for? I just want my money back."
>
> The guard says in a quiet voice, "Bob, do you see all of those people behind me? You are scaring them. Do you want to scare

them? What about Beth? Does she deserved to be frightened?"

The customer begins to realize the scene he has caused and calms down some. "No, I guess not."

The guard continues, "Thanks, Bob. I really appreciate it. Now, when you bring back the receipt we will process that return straight away and get your money back. We need that receipt for the transaction number, the amount you paid and a whole lot of other information. It is really important." The guard starts walking the customer towards the door. "So when you come back with that receipt ask for the Manager. His name is Mike and he will be more than happy to take care of you. I'll let him know to expect you."

As the customer exits he says, "Thank you."

The security guard smiles and waves. "My pleasure, Bob. Have a great day."

In this example, rather than take the bait presented by the irate customer, the security guard ignored the insults and instead focused on providing solutions. The guard never said, "No," which is often an escalating trigger word. When people want something, they do not want to be told, "No" or that they cannot have it. Rather, the guard redirected the conflict to focus on the requirements for a resolution. The receipt was no longer a block to a refund, but rather a solution to the refund. The guard implemented a number of calming and deescalating verbal techniques (using his name, making him aware he was frightening innocent people, etc.) and escorted him out of the store without a physical altercation. If at any time the irate customer physically attacked the security guard or the sales associate, it would have been unprovoked and the guard would have had the right to claim self-defense when containing and arresting the customer for battery.

# Assault Elements

After a force-on-force encounter, the security guard should notify law enforcement as soon as it is safe to do so. If the aggressor has been contained and arrested (as opposed to escaping), the security guard **must** notify law enforcement and request they respond to take custody of the arrested suspect.

It is best practice to notify law enforcement after any physical encounter, even if the suspect escaped. It is common for criminals, after escaping, to call law enforcement and report reckless, abusive or dangerous behavior by security staff. Being the first to call 911 ads credibility to the security guard's side of the story should law enforcement respond.

Often, even after being arrested, frisked, and sitting in handcuffs, suspects sometimes proclaim their innocence to responding law enforcement that the arrest was unlawful and/or the containment employed excessive force. Therefore, the security guard must be able to articulate the reasons for grudgingly entering into a force-on-force encounter and the reason for the arrest to the responding officer. The explanation must include three (3) key elements to legally justify the use of physical force. These are known as the Assault Elements. If a single element is absent, the security guard may be seen as the aggressor or willing participant in a fight and face possible criminal prosecution.

Timing is critical to the Assault Elements. All three Elements must be immediately present at the time the force-on-force encounter occurs. Past events or vague threats of a future occurrence are not sufficient cause to warrant a physical confrontation.

*All three (3) elements must be <u>immediately present</u> at the time the force-on-force encounter occurs.*

Assault Elements
1. Means or Ability
   The tools or skills readily accessible to commit the crime.
2. Opportunity
   The conditions immediately favorable to commit the crime.
3. Jeopardy (imminent peril)
   The reasons why the victim felt threatened at that moment.

If even a single element is missing, the legal requirement for lawful use of force will be found lacking.

Again, all three (3) elements must be present in order to physically protect yourself or others.

# Means or Ability

The aggressor must have the tools or skills readily accessible to commit the crime. If a drunken person proclaims he is "going to shoot everyone in the building," but has no firearm, lethal force cannot be used against him. If the man has no weapon to carry out his threat, then he does not have the means *at that moment.* The incident should be reported to law enforcement because this drunken man may indeed be serious and may leave and return with a weapon with which to carry out his threat.

The key is *readily accessible.* The means must available *at the moment* in order to take action. A threat of a future action does not meet the requirement to use physical defense.

A weapon is not required to determine means. If someone threatens with an empty-handed physical attack and it is apparent he is physically fit enough to do it, then it can be deduced that he has the means. However, if this person is so drunk that that his uncoordinated strikes will do little damage, full force defense cannot be used because the drunk simply does not have the means to effectively carry out his attack. This premise applies equally to teenagers, women or anyone at less than full capacity.

# Opportunity

The aggressor must have the conditions immediately favorable to commit the crime. Is the person in a position to harm? Is he screaming from across the street, is he in the same room, or is he in within touching distance?

Someone may have the means and intent to harm, but may lack the opportunity because of distance. If a disgruntled employee calls on the phone and says he is going to kill someone, and that he has a gun in hand, a security officer cannot grab a shotgun and drive over to the perpetrators house and try to shoot him before he can shoot the named victim. If the disgruntled employee were standing before the security officer, with a gun, and announced his intent to kill the security officer, then that guard has all three elements present and can do whatever it takes to protect himself or herself, even lethal force, in this case. However, for the personal calling on the phone the element of opportunity is lacking. Certainly, take the threat seriously, but the correct procedure would be to call the police. Such a threat comes under the heading of "criminal threats" in most states.

# Jeopardy (Imminent Peril)

The third Assault Element is the belief that the defender was in imminent peril. The defender must be able to explain, in clear and simple terms, why he or she felt the attacker was going to inflict serious bodily injury. Prior experiences, especially if they involve the attacker on previous occasions, body language, verbalizations and combative training, can all be used to express why the defender's life was believed to be in jeopardy.

It would be nice if all attackers expressed in a clear, loud voice for all to hear, "I am going to inflict grievous bodily harm upon you, Jack!" Reality, unfortunately, is hardly ever this fair. Therefore, in order to express to responding law enforcement, and potentially a jury, why we were concerned for our lives, we must identify those triggers and remember them. The challenge is that they appear and disappear quickly, are usually seen only by the defender, and "eyewitnesses" are usually totally unaware they are even occurring.

Although it is impossible to predict what another human being will do with accuracy, it is possible to recognize pre-assaultive characteristics. Other than surprise attacks, suspects will often display conflict indicators (unintentionally announce their intended actions) through some kind of gesture or body language. Numerous conflict indicators are ingrained into humans at a biological level. Many indicators also transcend verbal language and cultures. Although training can reduce or eliminate telltale signs (such as professional fighters, soldiers, competitive martial artists and gang members), the average person will be unaware of projecting intent to physically harm the intended target. That grants the well-trained defender the opportunity to take self-protective measures.

NOTE:    The following indicators apply mostly to "average" or "normal" people. Those who suffer from mental disorders, traumatic brain injury, or are under the influence of drugs or alcohol may act in random and unpredictable ways, sometimes attacking with no pre-assaultive indicators at all.

# Conflict Indicators, Verbal

### Profanity
The overuse of profanity, especially when specifically directed at the security guard, is an assault indicator. Liberal use of profanity demonstrates that the suspect is losing control. When mental control is lost, a physical response is imminent.

Profanity is also used as a distraction. A verbally harsh, racist, sexist, or attack upon the heritage of the security guard can shock or stun. The average individual is unaccustomed to personal, vitriolic verbal assaults. The average person will lose focus and concentration, thinking of the words and an appropriate response. That pause to think interferes with situational awareness and listening. Much that is said or done after an overly abusive vocal assault is completely missed. That is when the suspect can launch an attack against the unprepared guard.

**Loud voice**
Often times an aggressive person raises his or her voice just prior to attacking. This is common when a person is angry, intoxicated, or suffers from a mental disorder.

**Threats**
If a suspect threatens harm, chances are that the individual will attempt to assault the intended victim. The intent behind a threat is to intimidate and force compliance. Threats are usually followed by a physical attack, especially if the suspect is a former convict or gang member, where all threats are reinforced with action.

**Shallow breathing**
Breathing changes when a person enters a fight or flight response mode. A sudden change in aggressor's breathing may indicate a looming attack.

**Unusual statements**
A person whose thoughts seem disorganized or who is hearing "voices" may suffer from a mental disorder. Examples statements are "They're following me" or "I work for the CIA" or "There are devices in my body." Such people may or may not be violent or criminally inclined. However, they are unpredictable in any situation, especially as stress increases. The best course of action, if possible, is to speak with the person in a calm manner while showing no fear. Even when situation is under control realize that anyone suffering from a mental disorder may ATTACK WITHOUT WARNING.

**Depression**
Anyone talking about suicide or hurting others, must be considered extremely dangerous. In law enforcement circles there is an expression:

"Suicidal usually means homicidal." Many people who want to commit suicide are too afraid to do it themselves, so they do something threatening where they know law enforcement or armed security will be forced to shoot them. This commonly known as "suicide by cop." Always remain alert and diligent around individuals who may be experiencing extreme depression due to a recent divorce, breakup with a lover, loss of a job, perceived injustices by the government, etc. This includes staff, clients, the general public, friends and even family.

# Conflict Indicators, Non-Verbal

A person's "body language" (non-verbal indicator) may often times reveal the next action. Subtle indicators can give advance warning of an imminent attack.

**Red flushed face**
Embarrassment or anger may cause flushing or reddening of the face and ears. Anyone who flushes during a confrontation is experiencing extreme emotion and is on his or her way to reaching crisis.

**Fixed stare**
A person who "stares you down" or "mad dog's" may be preparing for an immediate attack. The predatory fixation is usually associated with the person about to make his move. This fixed stare can also be drug induced.

**Rigid body**
An escalating conflict can cause the body to dump vast amounts of adrenaline into the system. Adrenaline restricts the body to gross motor skills and the body tends to stiffen up. In a real life-and-death conflict few people are relaxed like they are in the training environment. Observing a person go rigid may indicate an imminent attack.

**Shaking, twitching hands, and clenched fist**
A person preparing to strike may appear nervous just moments before launching the attack. A shaking hand or the clenching of a fist may be the only warning sign.

Real-world example: A suspect acted like he was going to sit down on the street curb as instructed by a police officer. As the suspect bent down, he hesitated for a moment and clenched his left fist twice. It was just enough of an indicator to alert the officer to the danger. The officer took one step back and pulled a canister of pepper spray from his gun belt. One second later, the 6'-2", 220 lb. man swung at the officer. Being prepared for the conflict, the officer sent a steam of Oleoresin Capsicum into his face, preventing an ugly fight and possible injuries to the officer and suspect alike.

### Hesitation
A person unsure of his next move, like an inexperienced fighter or criminal, may come across temporarily as indecisive and hesitant. For example, a robber you may have just decided to harm the victim as well, and is inwardly thinking it over. It is common to have a suspect appear relaxed at first, then as the officer or guard nears discovering the suspect's drug stash or weapon, the suspect becomes "squirrelly" and combative.

### Irrational behavior
Anyone displaying extreme behavior such as hysteria, fear, derangement or anger should be considered a potential threat.

### Under the influence
Most combative situations also involve the suspect being under the influence of drugs or alcohol. With enough exposure to the drug culture it is easy to determine when someone is under the influence. The challenge is remaining safe and unharmed until that experience is gained. Each drug alters the mind differently and there are many different drugs available to abuse. It is impossible for this lesson to fully address this topic. What follows are some key lessons and indicators to remember:

- It is generally possible to determine if somebody is under the influence of a controlled substance by looking into their eyes: Either the pupils will be extremely constricted (2.0 mm or lower such as with opioids) or extremely dilated (6.5 - 7.0 mm with stimulants such as cocaine).

- Someone using amphetamines is going to exhibit paranoia, nervousness, and often violent behavior.

- Individuals on hallucinogens are going to be disconnected displaying such behavior as running around naked, "hearing" and "seeing" things that are not there, a look of fright or panic, and a "distant" look in the eyes.

- Some drugs, such as PCP (phencyclidine), can make the user immune to pain, grant superhuman strength and make the user intensely violent. If the suspect is known to be on PCP, do not approach or confront. Call for law enforcement immediately and clear the area of bystanders.

Marijuana and cocaine and are the most frequently used illegal drugs in the world.

A key factor to remember is that someone on drugs or alcohol is UNPREDICTABLE.

**Appearance**
Teenagers are notorious for saying, "people should not be judged by the way they dress or look." However, a wealth of information can be gleaned from a person's appearance. There is an expression in law enforcement: "If you look like a duck, walk like a duck, and talk like a duck, you're probably a duck." Gang members dressed in gang garb and "tatted out" (covered in obvious tattoos), when approached by law enforcement often whine, "Why are you harassing me?" They might as well wear a big sign that reads, "I'm a gang member." Apparent prison type tattoos should also cause red flag warnings. The reason is that traditionally people who go to prison are in gangs, or hang around gangs, or often engage in criminal activity. It may not be true of everybody, but when it comes to personal protection, protection of others and protection of property, play it safe.

It is nice when some people "warn" you of their personality (bikers, skinheads, racists, etc.) with subculture attire and ornamentation. However, there are those who select specific clothing to "blend in" that will give little, if no warning at all. They wear these clothes like costumes. FBI studies have concluded that many bank robbers wear baseball caps and sunglasses, or a bright colored piece of clothing to create a distraction when robbing banks. Sometimes attire can be used to deliberately hide criminal intent in plain sight as when bank robbers wear business suits.

Attire should never be the sole reason for watching a person. However, it is reasonable to consider a person's attire and body art when building a behavioral profile. Attire should never be the sole reason for consideration, but it can be added as a factor to the entire profile.

# One Equals Three

It is always bad to jump to conclusions. What follows are hypothetical scenarios.

An off-duty police officer enters a bank in normal "street" clothes to conduct business. As many off-duty officers do, he is carrying a concealed firearm. He drops his deposit slip and while bending over to pick it up, his sidearm is made visible to the patron standing behind him. The patron is presented with a problem. The man before him, whom he does not know, has the means to rob the bank (a firearm) and the opportunity (he is inside the bank). However, the patron is not justified in tackling the armed man before him as there is no third element of jeopardy (imminent peril). The armed man is in the bank legitimately and peacefully. Furthermore, there were no signs posted prohibiting firearms.

In a similar scenario, what if the location was a passenger aircraft? Is the armed man a Federal Air Marshal or a terrorist? Again, being armed on an aircraft gives the two elements of means and opportunity for terrorism, but jeopardy (imminent peril) is still lacking.

In either scenario, the situation changes when the man on the aircraft yells, "I am taking over this plane!" or the man in the bank yells, "Everyone on the ground, this is a robbery!" With those statements, a visible weapon and location, all three assault element requirements have been met and action can be legally taken.

Knowing and understanding the assault elements grants the ability to articulate to responding law enforcement why the actions taken were justified. Law enforcement, as well as employer and other regulatory agency, notifications must be made after every physical confrontation. All statements and reports should clearly note the assault elements as part of the justification in use of force. Those reports are legal documents and may be used in court as evidence in either or both criminal and civil trials.

# The Assault Elements Venn Diagram

Only in the intersection of all three assault elements (sets) can an individual use physical force to defend oneself or others.

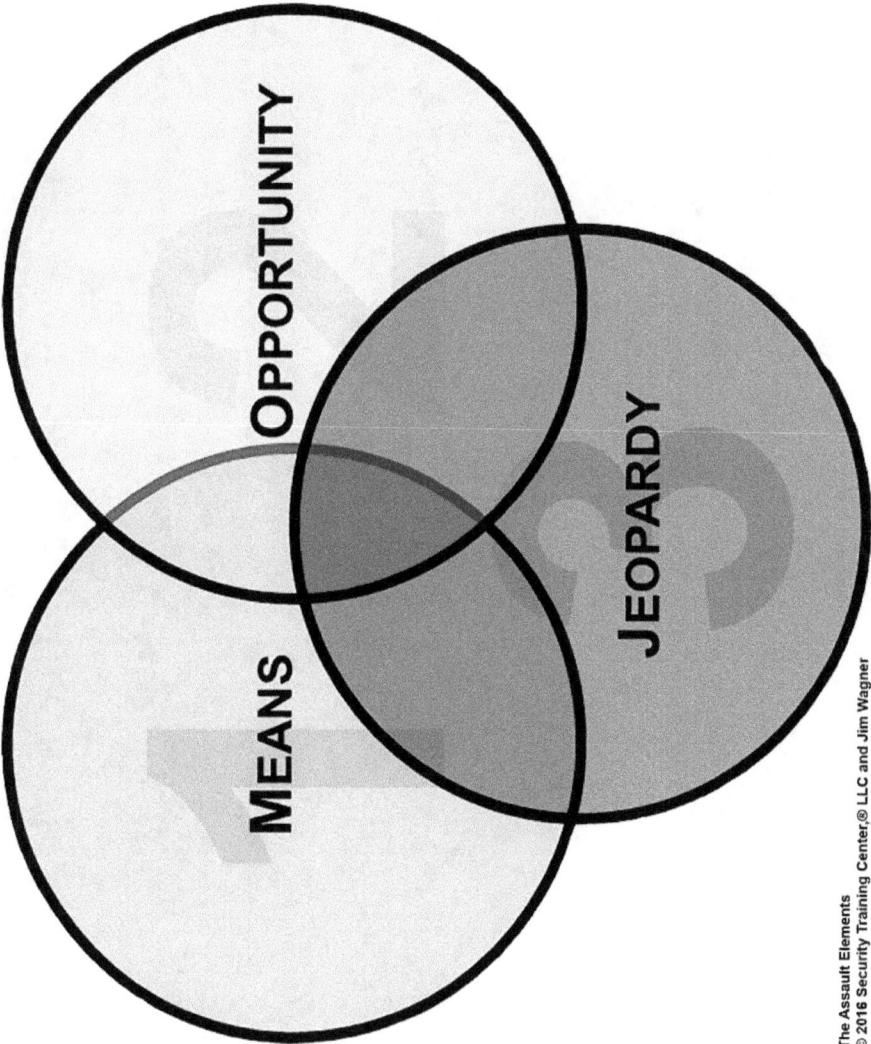

The Assault Elements
© 2016 Security Training Center,® LLC and Jim Wagner

OPPORTUNITY

JEOPARDY

MEANS

# The Use-of-Force Ladder™

Not every adversary is going to have the same level of fighting skills and the same reasons for fighting. Human conflict is unpredictable due to the countless factors involved. Yet, with the way most self-defense instructors teach their students how to handle a fight, one would come to the conclusion that there always is one generic attacker, and he is always the worst case scenario bent on your destruction. Yes, there are some predators out there who would not hesitate to victimize anyone they cross paths with, but a "cookie cutter approach" to dealing with conflict can result in physical harm and legal trouble.

Never forget that everyone is held legally responsible for their actions. This holds true for any force-on-force encounter. Whether a seasoned street cop, a third-lesson martial artist, or a security guard with 20-years' experience, some prosecutor or defense attorney is going to bring up the use-of-force issue. The defender is going to struggle if he or she cannot clearly articulate the different levels of force, and what can and cannot be done legally at each level. Thus, it is imperative that everyone understands the appropriate responses to a conflict.

# Based on Standards

Whether a soldier, jailer, street cop, SWAT officer, diplomatic bodyguard, counterterrorist agent, security guard, or "soccer mom," everyone must follow a Use of Force policy. Generally, the defender is protected when staying within the standard. On the other hand, straying outside of the guidelines (using unreasonable force), may result in criminal charges (jail or prison) and/or paying out hefty penalties in a civil law suit.

Security guards are not isolated from the law and are technically standard citizens. They are not granted the same leniency or use of force policies as law enforcement or the military. The citizen's use of force policies are far more restrictive. Ignorance of the laws is not a legal excuse that offers any protection, especially when it comes to excessive force cases. Please, forget everything seen on television or movies regarding use of force. Whatever is shown on the screen is for storytelling purposes, NOT EDUCATION, and is as far from reality as werewolves, vampires, and unicorns. Most civilian martial artists have no idea just how much trouble they can get into legally, even when they, in good faith, were just trying to protect themselves or someone else. There are a few well-meaning martial artists sitting in prison because they did not know where to draw the line, or even where the line was in the first place, when it came to the use of force. Although "the ladder" is similar in concept to what the military and law enforcement agencies must follow, the Use-of-Force Ladder for Civilian Self Defense™ is specifically designed for average citizens.

# Components of the Ladder

Like a real ladder that one leans against a building, the most stable place to be is not on the ladder at all. Once on, there are risks; injuries are possible even from a foot off the ground. Likewise, in daily life, it is always safest to avoid conflict. Yet, trouble can sometimes find us even when we are not looking for it.

Notice that the left arrow of the graph starts at the bottom of the ladder as a low risk situation then escalates to a high risk situation, while the arrow to the right starts from being cautious to being engaged in physical conflict.

The higher the ladder is climbed, the more unstable it becomes; especially when climbing alone. If other trained staff are present they can provide support (strength in numbers). Going beyond the ladder leads to death or serious injury, just as stepping off the top rung of a real ladder can lead to death or serious injury. This is indicated by the black tops of both arrows. It is imperative to always maintain control, no matter the level.

Notice that the two arrows in the graph point both upward and downward. This indicates that a conflict may start at any level, at any time and can move in either direction. It is possible for a conflict to initiate in Code Red without going through all of the previous rungs first. For example, bank robbers barge into the facility, blasting away with their guns. It is an instant Code Red.

Some situations may climb the ladder progressively, escalation, and in other situations what may have started off high, gives opportunities to deescalate.

Always attempt to diffuse, to deescalate, a conflict. A physical response is always a last resort.

# The Colors of Conflict

Notice that to the left of the ladder are the suspect's actions (aggressor), indicated with an extended gray triangle, and a vertical arrow next to it with a gradient of colors. The arrow corresponds with the Jim Wagner Conflict Color-Code System, inspired by my military, corrections, and law enforcement standards:

1. Secure (White)
2. Caution (Yellow)
3. Danger (Orange)
4. Conflict (Red)

STC Guard Card Training*

**Secure (White)** – This is staying off the ladder all together. This level is a secure place: home, work, social events, etc. Conflict is not anticipated. However, this does not mean complete security. Even at Code White there must be emergency plans in place in the event that the peace is disturbed. For example, when at home, there should be some sort of home security plan: locks, outdoor lighting, alarm system, surveillance cameras, escape routes, etc. At work, there should be have a reaction plan in the event of a workplace violence incident, robbery, etc.

**Caution (Yellow)** – This is the level maintained in public. Always be aware of the environment: people, vehicles, behind large objects, dark areas, etc. This is not a state of paranoia, but prudent caution known as *Situational Awareness*. This is why the arrow extends below the ladder and into the white area. A security guard must be alert long before any conflict arises.

Once there is any indication of a conflict, the yellow color blends rapidly into orange. On the ladder the yellow turns darker when a subject is giving VISUAL INDICATORS, such a hard stare (mad dogging), posturing, wearing gang colors, etc.

**Danger (Orange)** – At this level there is a real possibility of danger since the suspect is giving VERBAL INDICATORS: direct threats, suspicious word choice, etc. The intensity of this Pre-Conflict phase can escalate or dissipate. The potential for conflict can be rapid, steady, or gradual. Although words themselves cannot physically hurt, words will determine the course of action. If someone is threatening harm, the three Assault Elements must be present before physical action is warranted: *means* (the wherewithal to harm you), *opportunity* (the immediate ability to harm you), and *jeopardy* (imminent peril; the sincere belief the suspect is going to inflict physically harm, whether implied [such as a robber with a mask and gun] or verbalized ["I'm going to kill you!"]).

**Conflict (Red)** – Here physical confrontation, or force-on-force, has initiated. This does not mean all self-defense techniques are available. There are many levels of conflict. Even in warfare there are differences: low intensity conflict (guerilla warfare, terrorism, etc.) and high intensity conflict (all-out war or limited actions). For example, someone who pushes the security officer is treated with a different level of force than someone who attacks with a knife.

# Climbing the Ladder

The Jim Wagner Reality-Based Personal Protection Use-of-Force Ladder™ has four (4) rungs to make use of force levels easy to remember.

**RULE:**    When responding to the suspect's actions, the response must always be equal, proportional and reasonable.

The left of the ladder lists the suspect's actions and the right of the ladder lists the security guard's response. Note that the responses are equal, level and proportionate for each rung.

Begin reading the ladder at the bottom. The ladder starts at the base, the most stable, and ends at Rung 4, an unstable and unpredictable height. *The suspect's actions always dictate the guard's actions.* It is best to stay off the ladder if possible. Yet, when confronting hostile subjects, there may be no other choice than a physical response.

Only climb the ladder if the suspect moves up first. When the suspect moves down a rung, the security guard's response must match the action by moving down a rung as well.

JIM WAGNER REALITY-BASED PERSONAL PROTECTION™

BASED ON THE
UNITED STATES
LEGAL SYSTEM

# USE-OF-FORCE LADDER™
## FOR CIVILIAN SELF-DEFENSE

| MURDER OR MANSLAUGHTER | HIGH RISK | UNSTABLE SITUATION | CONFLICT | LIMITED OPTIONS |
|---|---|---|---|---|
| | | DEATH | | |
| | | SERIOUS INJURY | | |
| **FELONY ASSAULT** | | **4** | | **DEADLY FORCE** |
| | | MINOR INJURY | | |
| **ASSAULT & BATTERY** | | **3** | | **REASONABLE FORCE** |
| | | THREAT OF INJURY | | |
| | | NO INJURY | | |
| **VERBAL INDICATORS** | | **2** | | **VERBAL DEFLECTION** |
| | | NO INJURY | | |
| **VISUAL INDICATORS** | | **1** | | **CONFIDENT DEMEANOR** |

| CONFLICT CUES | | | | MULTIPLE OPTIONS |
|---|---|---|---|---|
| **SUSPECT'S ACTIONS** | LOW RISK | STABLE SITUATION / THREAT ASSESSMENT | CAUTION | **YOUR REACTION** |

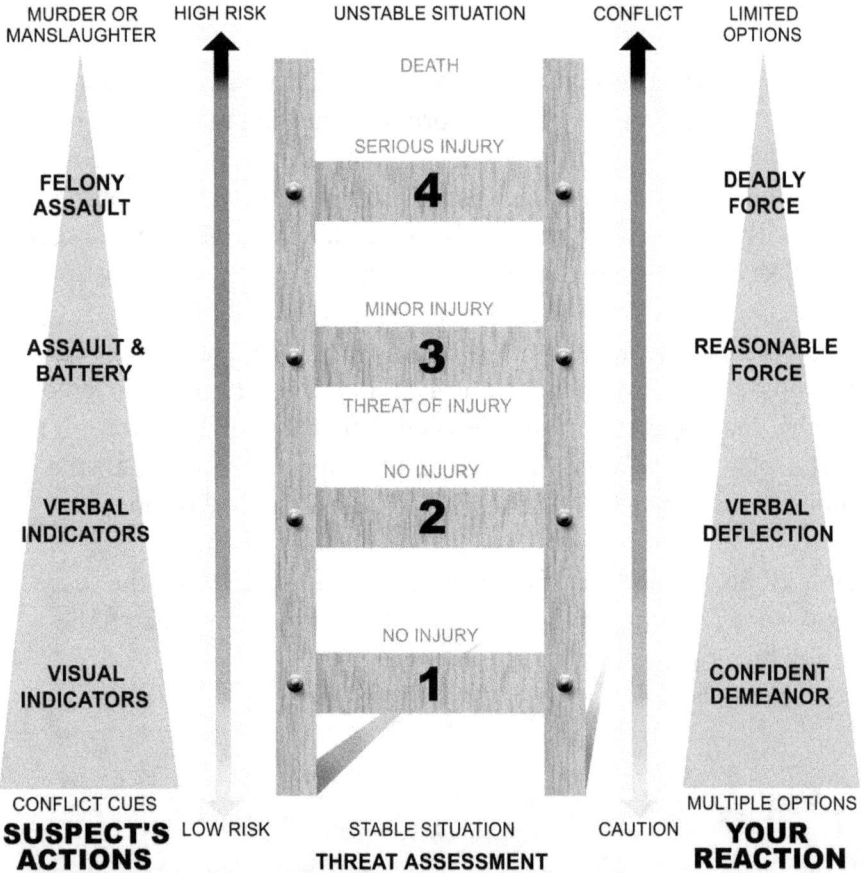

**DEADLY FORCE:** Any force that is likely to cause death or serious bodily injury.
**REASONABLE FORCE:** The level of force that a reasonable person would use in a similar situation.
**VERBAL DEFLECTION:** Words, or silence, used to diffuse a situation rather than to incite.
**CONFIDENT DEMEANOR:** Physical appearance of self-confidence and determination.
**THREAT ASSESSMENT:** Anticipating likely conflict paths before they occur (at all levels).
© 2003 Jim Wagner - Created and Designed by Jim Wagner   www.jimwagnertraining.com

# Rung 1

At Rung 1 the suspect uses VISUAL INDICATORS. In other words, the security guard feels there is possible danger based upon observations: a suspicious person approaching, somebody who is looking around nervously, a car slowing for no apparent reason. At the moment no laws are being broken by the suspect, but the guard intuitively feels something is off, and so mentally prepares for all possibilities.

The appropriate response is a CONFIDENT DEMEANOR (see YOUR REACTION under the right gray triangle). This means that looking confident and not afraid. Facial expressions indicate that awareness of the environment. CONFIDENT DEMEANOR also means that appearing prepared for an encounter or aware of the danger.

# Rung 2

At Rung 2 things heat up. The suspect is actively engaging the guard, or others, through VERBAL INDICATORS. This can be anything that warns that an attack is a distinct possibility, but short of direct threats. The conflict cues can be anything from the suspect's tone of voice to implied threats, or even things overheard, such as suspicious passengers in an airplane whispering about how "this is going to be a short flight." Those are not alarming words in and of themselves, but with some visual indicators one might suspect a possible terrorist attack.

If a suspect is trying to pick a fight the best thing to do is to try to calm that person down or ignore them altogether. This is known as VERBAL DEFLECTION. Reacting in this manner will not escalate the situation any further. However, some situations may require firm, confident verbal interaction.

Some circumstances may require verbal intimidation to diffuse an aggressive suspect. Intimidation should be used with extreme caution as if it is applied inappropriately, it can also be inflammatory and result in an escalation of aggression. The guard must use his or her best judgment for any given situation.

Words will not physically hurt, but they are often a good indicator if the encounter will escalate to a physical confrontation. Remember that threats of violence should be taken seriously. If threatened with battery, the security guard should be both mentally prepared and in position the respond to a physical attack.

# Rung 3

Rung 3 enters physical contact with the suspect. It may be a precursor push, or a punch, or even a sexual touch (sexual battery). This level where most martial arts systems teach the cookie cutter approach. For example, for a simple push to intimidate or anger, the guard cannot launch a side kick blow out the knee out, then come crashing down with a drop knee to the spine. Even though there is a right to defend oneself, the guard would most likely going to jail as this would be "unreasonable force" for the situation. The response was not proportionate to the initial event (the push).

Injuries are possible at Rung 3, but they are neither serious nor life threatening. For example, a broken nose, cuts, bruises, scrapes, soreness, etc. If the suspect throws a few swings because he is being ejected from of a club, the guard cannot rip his head off. The law will not tolerate that, even if minor injuries were sustained from his blows. Because there are no hard and fast rules on what can and cannot be done in a self-defense situation, the law applies a simple test: **What would a reasonable person have done in the same situation?** The responding law enforcement knows what is reasonable or not, and a jury who listens to testimony will determine what is reasonable or not.

# Rung 4

At Rung 4 death or serious bodily injury is likely to result, whether the suspect's, someone you are trying to protect, or yours. If a suspect does attack where death or serious bodily injury is likely to result (FELONY ASSAULT), then the guard has the right as a citizen to use DEADLY FORCE. This not only applies to felony assaults against the guard, but those the guard is hired to protect. If someone is trying to harm a family member, patron, or coworker in the guard's presence, the guard may (but is not required to) use deadly force. If the case goes to court, the guard will still be judged based upon the reasonableness of the force applied.

Examples of felony assault include attempted murder, mayhem (putting out an eye, severing a limb, ripping off an ear, etc.), rape, caustic chemical attack, robbery, etc. In other words, and remember these words carefully, ***there must be an immediate and unavoidable fear for your life, or the life of another.***

Notice that the gray triangles start off with broad bases, then taper off to mere points. The right triangle represents the options available in a conflict situation. Starting off with Rung 1, there are multiple options: walk away, call the police, yell for help, etc. However, by the time the guard is engaged in a life-and-death conflict, Rung 4, options are limited.

# Skipping Rungs

Skipping rungs on a real ladder makes the climb more hazardous. Unfortunately, in a real conflict, the guard may have to skip a rung. For example, the guard has a VISUAL INDICATOR that a man is strapped with a belt bomb. Although it is impossible to truly know the intention of another the person (it could be a prank for all anyone knows), the "bomb" itself implies intent to blow himself, and anything around him, up. Thus, in this example, the guard can go directly from VISUAL INDICATOR to DEADLY FORCE skipping REASONABLE FORCE altogether based upon observed behaviors and other non-verbal indicators.

# The Conflict Cycle

All human conflict has a predictable cycle. Whether the conflict involves a heated argument with a hostile suspect, taking down a terrorist in a life and death situation, or containing a violent clinical health patient, the cycle is always the same and always proceeds in sequential order. The type of conflict, and how an individual deals with the inherent stresses, determines the time and intensity spent in each phase of the cycle. Training, understanding and experience can reduce the time spent in each phase.

# JIM WAGNER REALITY-BASED PERSONAL PROTECTION™

# THE CONFLICT CYCLE™

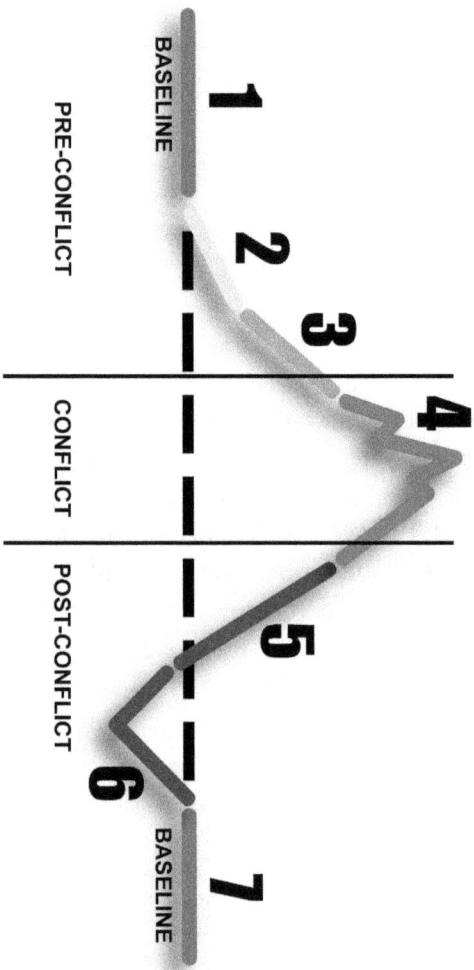

BASELINE | PRE-CONFLICT | CONFLICT | POST-CONFLICT | BASELINE

1 2 3 4 5 6 7

1. **EDUCATION** Knowledge Domain (preparation for conflict through training)
2. **INITIATION** The event that starts a conflict (conflict cues)
3. **ESCALATION** Immediate or gradual increase of danger (indicators)
4. **CONFRONTATION** Use of force (Jim Wagner Use-of-Force Ladder™)
5. **STABILIZATION** Escape or citizen's arrest, triage/first aid, police contact
6. **NORMALIZATION** Possible hospitalization, contemplation and litigation
7. **EVALUATION** Debriefing and learning from experiences; adjust training

The Conflict Cycle graph is divided into three components: Pre-Conflict (before the conflict), Conflict (whether visually, verbally or physically), and Post-Conflict (after the conflict). Within each section are numbered and color coded lines.

The numbering and color code system of The Conflict Cycle are detailed elements within each conflict component. Although actual conflict is a seamless event, the individual lines help to explain specific events that will take place within the timeline. This not only helps in understanding what to expect in a real fight, should one come, but how to better analyze what transpired in a logical sequence after the conflict (after action).

The Baseline, indicated on the graph by a black dashed line, extends to infinity in both directions. It represents normal daily life without conflict. The baseline represents normal behavior, thought patterns, and habits *before the conflict*. It is constant, but may adjust up or down after the event, depending upon the severity of the incident.

For example, if an individual is raped, after stage 6 (post-conflict) the individual may never regain the original baseline. Therefore a new baseline is established below the original baseline.

# 1. Education

The green line that sits on the baseline represents our preparation before a conflict. Everybody prepares for a conflict one way or another. Not preparing for a conflict is still doing is a personal choice.

Although it is impossible to predict the future, it is possible to prepare for the types of conflict that a security guard is most likely to face. The type of conflict likely to be present, called a threat profile, depends upon the post. For example, working a bank will have a different threat profile than working as a doorman at a trendy nightclub. Thus, the risks and the dangers will differ in nature and intensity from post to post. Proper preparation will help meet the challenge if faced with a conflict.

# 2. Initiation

The yellow line corresponds with the color code system and Use-of-Force Ladder, and indicates CAUTION. Conflict does not just happen, there is a starting point. Sometimes it is possible to see it coming, and other times it will be instant. The more familiar the guard is with the environment and threat profile, the more likely the guard will spot the initial conflict phase (conflict cues). For example, a man walks into a bank wearing a baseball cap and sunglasses. He performs a 60degree scan of the area before entering. His actions may indicate he is about to do a bank robbery. Initiation can be as simple as someone scanning the room, or as complex as a couple of terrorist making subtle hand signals.

# 3. Escalation

After initiation there will be escalation, which is represented by the orange line. Orange means that a conflict is imminent. Escalation can be immediate, such as a terrorist pulling a box cutter from a waistband, or gradual where somebody raises his voice. How far the escalation goes up the Use-of-Force Ladder depends on the nature of the conflict. Sometimes the guard will be able to diffuse an escalating situation, and other times the guard will have no choice but to respond physical. Just as in the initiation element, hopefully training and experience is enough to detect the escalation and prevent the event from reaching crisis.

# 4. Crisis (Physical Confrontation)

This is the phase where physical conflict takes place and it is represented by the color red (for danger). The line fluctuates within the range, as crisis can increase and decrease within the single event. If the guard's training closely parallels the incident, he or she should be prepared for it. If the training was unrealistic it could prove disastrous.

Notice the red line extends slightly into the Post-Conflict component. This is because the guard is not truly safe until the attacker is no longer a threat (escaped, contained or incapacitated). Even if the suspect fled the scene, did he really flee or is he just going around the corner to retrieve a weapon and double back? Therefore, one must still stay alert even after the initial hostilities have ended. Another example is a suicide bomber. The guard and patrons may have survived the blast, but should still clear the area in case there is a second suicide bomber who plans on killing the first responders.

# 5. Stabilization

The gray line begins the Post-Conflict phase; the color is gray because there may be uncertain variables at this stage (gray area). Now that the conflict is over, how is the suspect handled? This is also a time for self-triage, self-first aid if there are injuries and potentially a hospital visit. If a crime had taken place (if it went to Level 4, Crisis/Confrontation, a crime has taken place), then there will be police involvement; the guard should always notify the authorities even if witnesses call the police as well. Employer and other management notifications might be required, followed by report writing (Incident Reports, Daily Action Reports, etc.).

# 6. Normalization

The severity of the conflict determines how far the guard dips below the baseline; represented by the blue line.

At this point the conflict is over and the guard's mind and body seek to return to its baseline (normal life). If serious injuries were sustained there can be hospitalization. Another casualty can be psychological health in the form of Post-Traumatic Stress Syndrome or Conflict Fatigue. Depending on how traumatic the conflict was the guard may experience fear, fatigue, regret, performance disappointment, depression, or any number of negative emotions. How long the guard stays below the baseline depends on a lot of things: general outlook on the situation, previous training and experiences, and access to a support group. Familiarity with conflict reduces time spent below the baseline. Experiencing time below baseline is normal, but too much time there can lead to mental health issues.

# 7. Evaluation

At some point life returns to "normal." The baseline is once again reached, or reset, and is subsequently indicated by a green line. For some, conflict it is a wakeup call, and an opportunity to adjust their training accordingly.

# Use of Force in Defense of Property

The California Criminal Jury Instructions (3476), Right to Defend Real or Personal Property states, "The owner or possessor of real or personal property may use reasonable force to protect that property from imminent harm. A person may also use reasonable force to protect the property of a family member/guest/master/servant/ward from immediate harm.

"**Reasonable force** means the amount of force that a reasonable person in the same situation would believe is necessary to protect the property from imminent harm." (para.)[1]

Use of lethal force is never justified in the defense of property.

---

1 CALCRIM No. 3476

# Use of Lethal or Deadly Force

**Definition Lethal or Deadly Force:**
That degree of force that a reasonable or prudent person would consider capable of causing death or grave bodily harm.[1]

**Definition of Grave Bodily Harm:**
A crippling injury.[2]

Taking a human life is the most serious action a person can take. Employing lethal force must never be considered lightly and every option should be exercised before making the decision to take a life is made. The use of deadly should only be considered as a last resort.

Lethal force is not restricted to firearms. Employing any number items could be considered lethal force including, but not limited to, firearms, batons, clubs, and bricks. At times, even empty-handed or martial arts techniques could be considered lethal force. For instance, in some circumstances stomping the head while the target is prone, attacks against an unconscious or incapacitated target, and lengthy chokeholds could be considered deadly actions. Lethal force considerations may

---

1   Ayoob, M. (Instructor/Expert). (n.d.). Judicious Use of Deadly Force [DVD]. United States: Police Bookshelf.
2   Ibid.

be applied after the fact if the target has an adverse reaction to a "less than lethal" defensive tool. For example, the target has a strong allergic reaction to a compound in tear gas or defensive spray and suffocates or using an electroshock weapon against a target who then falls and sustains a lethal blow to the head.

Deliberate use of lethal force is only appropriate in a narrow and extremely specific set of circumstances: When there is an *immediate and otherwise unavoidable danger of death or grave bodily harm to the innocent.*

A critical component of the appropriate circumstance as outlined above is "immediate and otherwise unavoidable." The danger must be present at the exact moment with no chance to avoid or escape. Vague threats or promises to commit an act in the future do not warrant taking a life. All Assault Elements: Means, Opportunity, and Jeopardy, discussed in the previous section, must be present.

The California Criminal Jury Instructions (505) state, "Belief in future harm is not sufficient, no matter how great or how likely the harm is believed to be. The defendant must have believed there was imminent danger of death or great bodily injury to (himself/ herself/ [or] someone else). Defendant's belief must have been reasonable and (he/ she) must have acted only because of that belief. The defendant is only entitled to use that amount of force that a reasonable person would believe is necessary in the same situation. If the defendant used more force than was reasonable, the [attempted] killing was not justified."[3]

There is never a duty to kill in private security. Lethal force should never be used to defend goods or property. A single human life, even one of a known criminal, is worth more than any product or building. The single, most important duty of any security guard is to protect human life.

---

3    CALCRIM No. 505

> If there is ever the slightest doubt, do not employ lethal force.

Steps must always be taken to prevent unintentional or accidental deaths as a result of a security guard pursuing his or her prescribed duties.  Should there be no immediate criminal prosecution, a civil lawsuit may be filed by the surviving family and the community may place political pressure on the District Attorney to criminally prosecute the death, even years later.

In the eyes of the judicial system, taking another's life, even in self-defense, is treated first as homicide. It is then upon the defender to justify the actions. Even the self-defense penal code section titles are telling. They are written as "Homicide is justifiable…"

---

**Case Study**

In May 2010, a suspect was chased out of a retail pharmacy and into an alley for shoplifting toothpaste and crayons. A pharmacy employee contained the suspect by placing the suspect in a chokehold. Three other men and an off-duty corrections officer (who drew her firearm) assisted in the capture. Despite verbal commands to submit, the suspect continued to resist the arrest and struggled to escape the containment. The retail employee held the chokehold too long and the suspect died from strangulation. As of December 2013, over three years later, the civil litigation (a $400,000 wrongful death lawsuit) was still pending and there were renewed calls for a criminal investigation and prosecution of the employee.

---

# Ceasing Use of Force

When the aggressor is incapacitated or submits to the security guard, use of force must stop.

The California Criminal Jury Instructions (3474), Danger No Longer Exists or Attacker Disabled states, "The right to use force in self-defense or defense of another continues only as long as the danger exists or reasonably appears to exist. When the attacker withdraws or no longer appears capable of inflicting any injury, then the right to use force ends." (para.)[1]

The security guard should never let his or her guard down. Gang members have been known to feign submission to lull security and law enforcement into a false sense of security only to launch a surprise attack.

Even though the use of force may stop, the conflict is not over until the suspect is contained and in restraints.

---

1    CALCRIM No. 3474

# Use of Force in Effectuating an Arrest

Never use more force than necessary to effectuate the arrest. Care must be taken to ensure the safety of the security guard, suspect, and any bystanders. When resistance to the arrest decreases, the use of force must be reduced to match the amount of resistance.

As noted above, when the suspect submits to the security guard, the use of force must halt. However, do not let down on the level of awareness. As mentioned earlier the suspect seeming to submit may be preparing an all-out assault in the attempt to escape.

Once the suspect is arrested and restrained, the security guard immediately becomes responsible for the wellbeing of that individual. Care must be taken to ensure the safety and health of the arrested and restrained individual.

Lethal Force may NEVER be used to effectuate an arrest.

# Arizona Revised Statutes, Title 13, Chapter 38, Article 7, §13-3881. Arrest; how made; force and restraint

A. An arrest is made by an actual restraint of the person to be arrested, or by his submission to the custody of the person making the arrest.
B. No unnecessary or unreasonable force shall be used in making an arrest, and the person arrested shall not be subjected to any greater restraint than necessary for his detention.

# Hawaii Revised Statutes Chapter 803, Arrests, Search Warrants, Part I, Arrests Generally. §803-7 Use of force.

In all cases where the person arrested refuses to submit or attempts to escape, such degree of force may be used as is necessary to compel the person to submission. [PC 1869, c 49, §7; RL 1925, §3973; RL 1935, §5406; RL 1945, §10707; RL 1955, §255-7; HRS §708-7; ren L 1972, c 9, pt of §1; gen ch 1985]

# Knowledge Check

1) Multiple Choice
Regarding Use of Force when making an arrest:

A)  Security guards are held to the civilian use of force rule set.
B)  The guiding principle for use of force is "necessary amount of force."
C)  The guiding principle for use of force is "reasonable amount of force."
D)  Both A and C.
E)  None of the above.

2) True/False
Lethal Force may be used to effectuate an arrest.

A)  True
B)  False

3) Multiple Choice
In order to legally defend oneself using physical force against a hostile subject which three elements must be present?

A)  Fear, Threat, Means/Ability
B)  Fear, Opportunity, Cause
C)  Means, Opportunity and Jeopardy
D)  Ability, Fear, Intent
E)  None of the above.

4) True/False
To use lethal force one must have an immediate and unavoidable fear for one's life, or the life of another.

A)  True
B)  False

# Knowledge Check
# Answers

4) A
3) C
2) B
1) D

# References

Anthony Kyser Death: Video Of Alleged CVS Shoplifter's Killing Prompts Call For New Probe. (2013). Retrieved from http://www.huffingtonpost.com/2013/01/18/anthony-kyser-death-video_n_2506106.html

Arizona Revised Statutes, Title 13 - Criminal Code. (2014). Retrieved from http://www.azleg.state.az.us/ArizonaRevisedStatutes.asp?Title=13

Ayoob, M. (1980). In the Gravest Extreme: The Role of the Firearm in Personal Protection. Concord, NH: Police Bookshelf.

Ayoob, M. (2014). Deadly Force: Understanding the Right to Self Defense. Iola, WA: Gun Digest Books.

Ayoob, M. (Instructor/Expert). (n.d.). Judicious Use of Deadly Force [DVD]. United States: Police Bookshelf.

California Penal Code. (2016). Retrieved from http://www.leginfo.ca.gov/cgi-bin/calawquery?codesection=pen

Hawaii Revised Statutes Chapter 703, General Principles in Justification. (2015). Retrieved from http://www.capitol.hawaii.gov/hrscurrent/Vol14_Ch0701-0853/HRS0703/

Hawaii Revised Statutes Chapter 803, Arrests, Search Warrants. (2015). Retrieved from http://www.capitol.hawaii.gov/hrscurrent/Vol14_Ch0701-0853/HRS0803/HRS_0803-.htm

Hawaii Revised Statutes, Division 5. Crimes and Criminal Proceedings. (2016). Retrieved from http://www.capitol.hawaii.gov/hrscurrent/

Judicial Council of California Criminal Jury Instructions. (2016 edition). New Providence, NJ: Matthew Bender & Company, Inc.

Shoplifter Dies From Worker's Chokehold, Cops Say There Won't Be Charges. (2010). Retrieved from http://www.huffingtonpost.com/2010/05/10/shoplifter-dies-from-work_n_569851.html

Wagner, J. (2004). The System for All Systems. Costa Mesa, CA: Jim Wagner Reality-Based Personal Protection.

www.ingramcontent.com/pod-product-compliance
Lightning Source LLC
LaVergne TN
LVHW051815080426
835513LV00017B/1956